T0368485

Seasons
of a Distinct
Passion

MICHELLE GARCIA

AuthorHouse™
1663 Liberty Drive
Bloomington, IN 47403
www.authorhouse.com
Phone: 1 (800) 839-8640

Published by AuthorHouse 03/20/2015

ISBN: 978-1-5049-0319-6 (sc)
ISBN: 978-1-5049-0320-2 (e)

Contents

*I*nspiration

Going through many phases in life growing up day by day, is what often helps me create and deliver, the rest would be upto you. In this book in particular; verses my last book The Strength with in. that one stayed a little closer to the heart; because it was mostly based on personal loss and self perseverance.

I hope you enjoy this book, as much as I did putting it together. I hope to show a little more growth in knowledge and experience; that may relate to others. With a little twist of fun

Growing With Reflection

In many ways, I am growing in a lost world, spinning insanely! Yet I know that my mistakes will be ok.

It is strange to see, myself in this hole, filled with dark shadows shaking all around me.

There seems to be no escape? although I attempt to rise up against this lost place.

This is not where I belong! And it would be wrong, if I refuse to see the shining light right above me.

The brightness is what Fullfills me, with kind aspects, just waiting for my arrival.

It is! Still quite sometime, till I find the strongest strand of survival, but you will always see my rivals.

'One Hit Made A Run For More'

I sit here, on my own, but I am strong, for as long as I have the grace in
my hands. The needs, to proceed in life's race is here for me.

I place my speed, on what is left for me to save, I make a call, but
it is he, who says when and how the shots can be made.

I will not plead my case, because what has been given is enough
for me, to see that this is one thing that is real.

My mind has many speeds, my heart many griefs, but my soul will lead with many deeds.

I plant these words that were handed down to me, and I plan never to take anything for granted.

Therefore, I will always sit slanted, I may be here just to entertain in my dismantled
ways, but I will handle time because this life is meant to be mine.

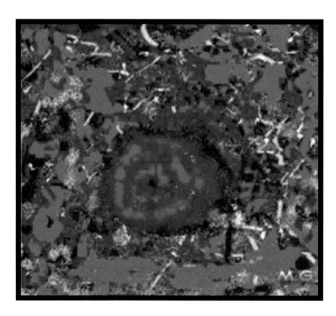

An Original Queen

I am here to stay, while the delayed has gone away.

i might of displayed; the misplaced, but i found new grace; with the rays all in my space.

Today is the day that I re-make and re-create who I am, and take down these mistakes, and wrongful says of me.

I am not for sale, nor will I be put up just to be stamped and mailed out.

When in doubt I am down, I will not keep a frown on this face.

In this place I was made to amaze, that alone I will not concede in my days, but I may stampede on mysterious games.

Where I'm from I am some of you, and some of me, but don't be fooled because I know I will complete.

$\mathcal{A}$ Healing Heart

A Broken heart can heal, no matter how many times it bleeds

Sometimes that is all it needs, to succeed towards where ever it should be.

A broken heart, will see its peak once again; sometimes we just have
to wait till it seeps down under at its weakest plead.

A broken heart may lead to seal itself, but it will heal indeed, it will see heat, and when
it has reached a need, we must yield, to take the time our heart needs to relieve

Most of us heal when we are concealed, but just wait and
see, one day a broken heart may soon be free.

Time may seem unreal, but we must reveal, what is real.

When we hurt the most, we should all take the time to heal, but when
times get hard, don't be alarmed, because we are bound to burn like darts
piercing through, after all; that is the art of a broken heart.

Our hearts may get stolen and then broken, but only time will
tell, that our heart will see hope once again.

The heart was chosen; and even when times have us frozen from being broken,
we must fight like crazy, because we were all meant, to love like a hopeless

A heart is not only meant to beat and bleed, but to love; without condition,
and when it breaks, it will seem like there wont ever be daylight, but a heart
is meant to be yours and it will always heal, with time and hope

$\mathcal{I}$ngression

Starting over; is better at risk towards a new beginning.

To achieve at something, is to complete, is to act in every attempt

To have knowledge, is taking guidance when it's offered to us.

And in order to go through acceptance is to admit when we have failed,

To comfort is to step up and help one another

'This is dedicated to everyone that has been there for me, through all aspect of life.

$\mathcal{M}$ysterious Plays Often Don't Stay

Smiling faces, shine upon me day in and day out.

Some of many colors, but most of them are just scholars! with high maintenance honors.

Little do they know, I can detect in their effects! But I will maintain
and play to ones defects, of their intents to fool and offend.

Although! I know what is being pulled, with ones distinct expression! Just; don't be
surprised! if I fill you with suppression, making your presence become extinct.

Yes Indeed, I will know a friend, from a pretended phony.

*T*ruth Always Stay's, Fakes Just Run Away

True Friends usually stay till the end, others are just there to
Pretend and then run away.

They send fake smiles to extend the suspense, and then they condemn you to walk that
extra mile suspending you from becoming content.

Friends stay a while and guard the paths, from these fakes.

Friends please come here and let's gain strength, to shake up these snakes, so these games
aren't done to gain fame.

'Those who are waited upon are not to be waited on, but those that are waited for may
wait for those that wait for them.'

Royal As Can Be

I am not grimy! Just a bit feisty, I might be shy, but my pride has me on high and mighty.

Smiling right, I'm so tight! Always, in disguise dusting off dirt I may find.

I sigh? And take my turns; some of you might like me! Or even try to fight me, but you can't bite me.

I am quite shiny! Just like ice, so fly and bright! Because I am cool just like that.

Stand Tall

"Never give your all! Because most people will make you fall.

But, if you get back up! After you've taken a fall, be sure and stand tall.

To make them stall! From having a ball, so that next time they may recall all of your falls and will haul away faster than a car."

Holding My Own

Word is; i might have been lonely, but I just wanted you to hold me,

Although, how could I hope, for something before me when I barely even held me.

I just started to show me, what it is to own me, to feel free and to devote to behold me.

So one day I could be whole; and lead towards whom ever may be the one for me.

Independent Soul

i am striving on my own, please leave me alone! I know that I can try on my own, just don't leave me alone pretty please?

I don't want to be controlled; I just need to be consoled! Sometimes I seem to loose my roam, but I am still grown.

Will you come hold me? I am not lonely, but will you please come hold me, so that I don't feel so lonely.

I am not that old, but I have been told, that I am a bit to bold, for my own soul, sometimes I feel so cold, but I am not made of stone.

I am strong in mind, but a little weak at heart just yet.

I hit hard with my hits, but it's only to leave an impact in my pitch.

I am always in need, it is what seeks, out loud, my speed is always on a steady streak, and I am free! But I still feel a need to be free.

I may turn out to be a bit weak, but my heart still makes a distinct sound,

I am passionately warm, lyrically garnished, and literally filled with actions; they are the main platter of my words.

'I am a need of a need, and I will not stop, until I am heard and set free.'

$\mathcal{T}$ruth

Love can not be controlled! It just grows unpredictably, when the heart knows what it needs.

Love is kind, but it will often blind, if someone is not careful.

Sight! can usually tell when it sees appeal, to want, although; that can also build up, to become something un-real.

Love is, meant to wind someone up, not to break them down.

Love! Never causes a frown, nor does It clown, and pound rounds of shots; To create scars for life.

Love is the brightest star! In the night sky, it is also the beautiful light in the sight of day

Love is, not meant to cause harm! But to be wrapped around someone's arms, filled with lovely sounds.

Love is, meant to be shown, not just said, in crumbled up words, not all of us can understand.

Love! Does not lie, or sigh, But it may often cry, when it does not shine.

Love, should never be rage or anger, although! It is sometimes pain; that one can not explain.

Love! should never be jealous, or to be left in vain, but it is meant to gain trust and patience.

Love is, meant to be a nation! Not a statement, if we could not complete! Then we all failed true love.

'I was touched creating this piece!'

Hope is, like a wishful dream.

True love, comes from deep with in our soul! As massive Flows of emotion reflect upon those we like to call our own

Some feel just right! And others may not, but who is to know? Until we have looked around, to find that special touch of light, love has to offer.

When that round! Comes to such a bound, lets hope! Who ever love may be, will bow down in bended knee.

Pleading with such need! Showing good deeds, and love for free.

People always say! Save the best for last, but even that might not ever come.

So when loves true word! Comes out to show, whether it be your first, second, or last; be sure you know there past, work with there present, and hope you two can live a wholesome future.

Kiss of a Dream

I should have never kissed you! Because now I just miss you, some how I can feel you, as if I read you.

Most days, I use to want to keep you! But now I need you in my speeds of life.

I always heal! When I hear you, but I become free when I see you.

Now and days, I don't want to awake, but it's only because I kissed you! And now I just really miss you.

Radiance

You are a bright source of a radiant light Shining upon me,
The bright aspects, you share with me, feel so real.

You show up in flairs! I can not compare, to no other, although I am just left to stare.

You Influence me daily, with the many assets you carry, transcending into volts of extravagance.

You and I may not be so merry each day, but I will always be here to stay, and I know you would do the same.

Therefore, I will hold your heart when it is broke and your mind when its speed is stole,

I will console your soul! When it is most in grief or disbelief, and I will lift your speech when it is most in need.

Your kindness is quite elite to me! And please believe that your guidance has left me in needs to succeed.

In these scenes, you see more in me, than ever could see in myself,

Yes indeed! You have been so neat to me, but I must say that I still can't believe that you have been sent to me.

I am blessed! With the most gifted, and trust I won't ever lift, nor swift it away.

For many days, I have wanted to compete, but I know that no matter how much I plead, it can't be me.

There may be many reasons, but regardless there will always be seasons with u and me, yes indeed I will always be back to complete you'll see.

'what matters, is when something true shines through.'

Simply Me

Simply me; I have much dignity, showing off supremacy for my vicinity.

Often living in serenity, but the deficiency is what overwhelms the intimacy.

I am in some kind of vacancy only because I am simply me, with so much meaning.

$\mathcal{I}$F

If I cried; would you dry my eyes?

If I sigh, would you be my guide.

If I fight, would you stay by my side?

If I show my pride, will you show me right from wrong?

If I try, would you let me buy some time?

If I lied me down to sleep, would you spend the night wit me, or just hide from my sight.

If I died, would you rewind your mind and remember times, that were filled wit so much kind.

So High

So high on speed, I lost my keys, but some how u say I lost my teeth.

Damn why you give me so much grief, just let me be, because I can't even get some sleep.

I am so high off this speed, I don't even need those keys, but will u help me; find my teeth,

"Sometimes; its ok just to say fuck it, just be careful you don't puck it too hard, for it to come back in reverse and fuck you up."

Non Sense

Sometimes I don't make sense, but don't take offense.

I just want to pass these tests, so I can stay blessed.

It has been said; that I could be one of the best, if I only made sense, but I'm just trying to be equal to the rest.

I may never make sense, but, I hope you don't get in defense, because I am just trying to do my best.

istorted

Distorted I was, tried so hard just to get sorted, but maybe I wasn't ready for it.

Somehow I felt un-kind; my sight was too much for my eyes to bare.

Sitting here without a moment to spare, forcing myself to share my mind, just because I care too much.

I stare un-absorbed; I often extend far from all I pour out.

When in-doubt I am in need of kind apportions, I feel as if I was zoned out.

My motions are distortions, of nothing but pure devotion.

I am always aware of my supported ones, regardless of my emotions, I feel so distorted from all these commotions.

'Giving too much is not getting too much, not getting too much is suffering too much, for giving too much and not getting too much.'

rought

Far into a drought, I'm left to part in doubt,
Somehow I lost count; of all the lines I have crossed.

Often forgetting what life is all about, I might sound crazy, but it can be amazing, how lives get racing.

So many rounds with such heavy pounds on my shoulders and all these routes I am constantly rushing threw crowds.

I'm not at a rest, but striving, for nested words to be at there best.

Intensely; thriving to let the drought end, because, it has left me in doubt.

Fadeless Rain

I've got pain written all over my face, I'm not a disgrace, but I am in full range of strange paces.

Caught up in distress, I am racing in place, but I must stretch to end this rain, that leaves me in vain.

The day that I am tamed, I hope my face does not fade away, just like these rainy days.

A Mindless Phase

Why does time play with my mind, spending so much might, trying to find what's meant to be mine.

I come to find I have such hard sighs, I can't even find what it is I'm searching for.

Obsessively blind through my eyes, but I am still kind.

Why does time play with my mind, maybe I just need to unwind for some time.

Can I find those lines; I like to write, so that I can reply in my rights, just too comfy in my sight.

May my might get some light, so that I become a delight, to all the time my mind can find.

ounded

So tired of running; squirming around swiftly, just to surround myself in a dark place.

I really need to rest my head; I am not at my best just yet. I am barely set on one end, but I bet it's only to exempt.

I dispense my time, because I have been there for many days to long, but how could I have gone wrong.

It seems like I have been brought to a mess, but my mind is what does not lay to rest.

I try to unbind every time, although this is a bind of my own.

So filled with speed, I am left to think how my mind has so much greed, not only to seal, but to keep me from sleep.

No wonder I can't ever sleep, there is so much speed running through my mind that I can never unwind for a little time.

I like to think that I am fine, but I am so blind, will some one please come find me, because i am afraid that I'm not fine.

Lost Wonders

Sometimes I wonder when my time froze, or where it even goes.

Did it flow, or did it just blow away, I often find myself on the go, but yet; I don't know where the day tow's off to.

I sigh; dragging my wheels on the ground day after day, I sometimes wonder, will I ever grow into something whole or will I just slow down and let this crown go.

I wonder will I live only to stay around to be at my bounds, or will I leave just to be in my rounds; and getting no where but in my frowns.

I sometimes wonder where my life will go, will my might continue to show, or will this fight know its end.

I sometimes wonder will I get to the next level, or will I stay in a dark hole.

Restless Nights

I rarely sleep at night, and I don't know why I fight my self to sleep most days.

It often feels as if I have stayed awake, all the way through, till day.

I don't take no sleep aid, although, this could be just a sleep phase.

From day to day, I tend to shake in tears, because I can not remember, when it all got started.

I use to know how to be regarded, now I say that I am here, just to get discarded.

An Empty Flow

Running on empty feels so heavy, I sometimes don't know what to say, but I do know! That, I don't want; to fade away.

I take time out, as if I was on a sideline, but everything seems to slide my mind.

Running on empty seems so scary, I carry my head up high, but I find no sign of what is mine.

I don't like to hide; but still it often plays with my time,

I must try, for not only what is right, but what feels nice too.

Running on empty is so daring, I don't even know what it is I should do.

Running on empty can be quite shaky, it looks to be free and simple, although it is very lengthy and dim full.

A Sense of Need

I scream for help! But no one hears me; maybe I am not so loud! Or am I just an empty sound?

I am constantly squirming through town, feeling so alone! But reality is I am not alone.

My dreams are what keep me restraint! It's no wonder why I can not sleep at times.

Still when I am awake, I feel as if no one sees me there.

Twirling in circles, I cry for help, hoping someone will come and save me.

I tend to hold in all the shame, but truth is no one is to blame.

I am filled with so much pain! "No one even knows my name".

Yelling for comfort! But it does not seek me yet.

What often takes me over are actions! That rapidly get erased.

I thought they all had gone away, but they come back; to haunt me over and over.

Now all that is left for me is a need! A need of protection.

Suddenly, I see no place for staying, nor is there for escaping, it feels like I'm going insane.

So I scream! For you, but I am afraid, you have other amends before me.

I am trapped in despair, with all that is stuck inside me, but still you put time on hold for me! And you come back to save me; every way that you can.

A Trite Delay

Sleep has finally caught up to me, I can barely see!
I am un able to speak, from all that I have seen.

Running on caffeine, throughout the day, I wonder how long, I will delay.

I will say that I have made my way, past three days.

Fast lanes have made me pay, for life's mess, but I will say that I have to take blame, for this crazed stress.

It's been a shame, that I have stayed the same, in this faze of many games.

Although, just to think! That I now just became free, to breath once again, and I am not only sustained, but I do remain destined for some kind of fame.

Now I have you to thank, for the most important have stayed true to my name.

I am finally relieving my pain, and re-setting my flame, how must I say, that my lack of sleep is what often helps me see this kind of release.

Hello, Sweet Dream.

Hello, sweet dream are you here to be my light?

Will you be my sight, when my day feels lost?

Hello, sweet dream, will you guide my sighs and heal my cry's?

Will you be there, to show me peace, and help me sleep at night?

Hello, sweet dream will you be there to protect my fights, when life gets hard?

Will you show me the love of my life, or do I not get that right?

Hello, sweet dream will you be my might, when I am laid to rest at the end of my days?

The Night Sky's Rise

The moon is so bright, it lights up my night, and it is strange that I am awake this late.

I find it hard to write, but the moon is so bright; the light shining upon my face, makes me want to rise!

Reflections of the night sky, sinks into my eyes, it reminds my mind of a sight I could have had, if I did not carry so much baggage.

The moon is so nice, it's hard not to have no one to make things right.

Although, the lit up night, is so amazing, just to have it shine upon my face.

The night sky, feels so right, it makes me want to rise up, just so I could touch the bright light.

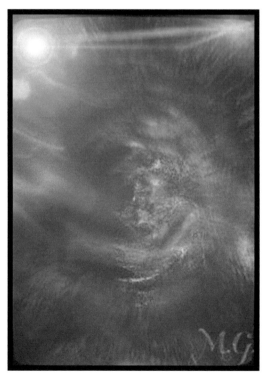

Presence

Your presence has always brought me hope, even when my essence does not glow.

Some how you flow with a powerful blow, centered deep within your soul, reflecting out and making something feel whole.

Your hope brings me strength. To cope with new strolls, but I still hold these jolts inside my moans.

Hope often, comes through and soaks up, most of my roars, giving me the deals, to heal.

Your beliefs, lead me towards the courage we share.

Feeding on strength, you leave me hope, to face another day.

Greedy Needs

So many speeds inside of me, going slow just isn't me.

My needs are not at a heed, although my speech might be asleep.

My mind is always in grief, feeding my emotions with greed, but I am not mean.

I am just use to these crazy speeds, that won't let me be, because I am always in need.

$\mathcal{I}$t's Been Raining

It's been raining all day and all night, it's sad to say I can't play outside.

Its so cold, I had to curl up in my sheets, just to believe that I am warm.

I can't deny that I feel so alone in this lingering rain; it's been raining all day and all night.

I try lying still, although, I am hesitant to say, that I am way too much in heat, to pass up this tease,

Temptation; in these teasing streams, I just can't help myself with urging senses.

For now, all I could do is moan in sighs, trying hard not to flow on my own.

Damn! I really need someone, but I must wait for this rain to subside.

It's been raining all day and all night, I cannot wait for this suppressing rain to end tonight

Subtle

So subtle watch me switch these gears, through the days I bet you wish you were here, instead of there.

You can't compare my flair, to the stare I put on your face, when you watch me race trough your space.

In a phase I move so quickly, you won't even know what hit you see, but I assure you won't miss my bliss

Now watch me shift and tilt this split, I make my switch in such swift ways you would think I was a game.

Creating; a maze, abbreviating your gaze, into believing, that I am this flame that came and blazed in your face.

So crazed; I disengage, just to leave you dazed and completely amazed.

"Sometimes you can do a lot with one word, such as one word can do a lot for you."

If You Must

Fill me up with your love, if you see a dove.

Fill me up with your hugs, if you have that kind of luck.

Fill me up with your passion, only if you come in fashion.

Fill me up with your lust, if you must, just don't bust my bubble.

Fill me up with your cuddles, but watch it, because I am that subtle.

I got puddles of blood, filled with love, so come give me a hug if you have that luck.

Fill me up with your lust, if you must, because I've got that love
that needs to be in puddles, of your passionate style,

Fill me up with cuddles, but watch your butt, because I am that subtle.

reams of Reality

Living my dreams, have led me to see many things, it is so amazing, to even be in this ring, but I bring my spring of speeds with me

Living my dreams, I can't believe I made this league, even if I never make royalty, I feel free as a queen.

There may have been streams of bleeds and pleads, but I am still me

Humble with kindness, but I still rumble and mind.

None the less I have stumbled on a few crumbles, but I can still move like a funnel.

Living my dreams can be refreshing, but it also can be quite depressing.

Sometimes there is rephrasing and other times it's just appraising.

It is the gracing of my race, that wont keep me from praising the one from up above.

He is the one for granting my dreams and showing me that love, is the life of my reality.

Persistent Speed

Dream, big and never give up, or let anyone rein on your goals, although, one must keep in mind that result, does not come in expected fashion.

You must have passion to go after your dreams, guidance to breath and strength to succeed.

I believe in my dream to live in speeds, I have got to see many things and receive plenty of means.

I can now say that I am living my dreams, even if I may never get to wear my ring, but yet, I still have the sting to believe it can be for me.

"its ok to dream big and love hard, till theres no more room left to fill"

Living, Loving, Lasting

They say I wouldn't make it past twelve, since then I have held myself through my trail

Now I am twice that age and I take the stage, to thank my parents for there unconditional love and caring support

I am aware that I have been blessed, sometimes I wish that I could share it with the rest.

I have past some hard tests, and yes there is more to come, where I am from I am meant to flood, whether it is love or blood.

I am not arresting, or detesting being a pest, but I am set to prevail.

It is he who can only derail my trail, so I must not stay frail to break in some kind of mistake.

I am not here to blame, but I will thank those that did not know, I may not be so stable, although I could be at a table of recorded proof.

I am a bit distorted, but that is what restores, the beauty of my soul.

Any one of these days I may go, but it is up to him, to say when it's time to come home.

I am known to be at my throne, carrying few thorns, but I will always go with a powerful flow.

Day to Day

Taking things, from day to day, can sometimes feel so grey.

I should say that sometimes they have to stay that way, so that I could remain safe and regain my strength.

May the day not end today, because safe can be so plain somedays.

I came to play this little game, I crave, but to crave is not the same without flame.

I must be brave, to have tamed the games, on some of these names that I have gained.

Maybe day by day! Isn't so safe, but it buys me time, to pace my stay.

I could say that safe, is now in my place, but I must make my way taking it play by play.

Even if no words are said, in my days, I know that everything will be ok, and I may return to win someday.

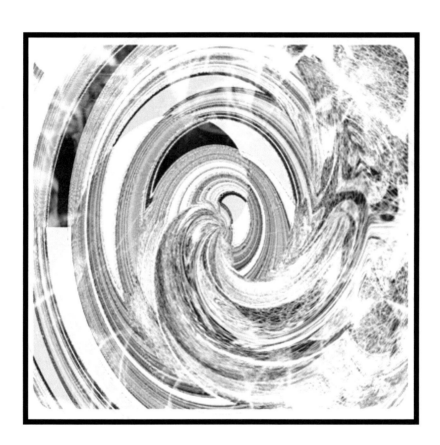

ilent Noise

My silence, speaks louder than my voice, but it is my voice that speaks in profound tones.

Speaking my sound, is like utterly, creating noise, just like the noise in my head.

Although, there is a silence, in my voice, that constantly speaks! Louder, than my own, words.

A Stumbling Ground

I have felt off balance, the past couple of days.

I am quite clumsy, and now I can't shake me awake.

I have had to make a few mistakes, just to shuffle my ways in place.

I came to stay, but my mind, just fades away.

I am at a loss for words, and I don't even know what move to make today.

Tomorrow may just be another day, but I still can't say, that I am bothered in any way.

Although, it does seem, as if I have a lost sorrow, but for now I
can only barrow some time to find some balance.

Still it is as if all I have are moments, to lavish.

I have not yet established, what I've wanted to say, or even what I have
needed today, but I can't complain because I am really ok.

I just have to notate, that I am not insane, just a little un-safe I'd say.

I take time to rotate, because I know I can relocate.

I am detained today, but the next day, I may reclaim to re-gain balance.

Re-framing, the emptiness inside, in order, to become enviously
astound, of my own crown because I will stay around.

acing My Run

I feel as if I were near the end of my days, but maybe it's because, my life is entering a new phase.

I am trying so hard, to move in a steady pace, but it only leaves me in a daze.

I can not save, for what is not my game, but yes the days are still gazing away.

Perhaps! I should begin racing, all over again; it is where my fame likes to stay.

Still, I can not; erase the pain that always has me going insane.

I was always known to play it safe, but I must have been born, to set a record strait.

Although, I can not correct, every mistake; that is, or has been made, the sustained is what keeps me sane.

The obtained, is what puts me back in this race, even though, I can not seem, to create my steps, it is, in my maze that I remain, at my best.

With Pride

My fight is over, I must now roll sober, I am not much older, but I do feel a bit colder.

Riding like a rollercoaster, had me driving wild, it has been miles of fast speeds and multitudes of heat.

Hard crashes have caused many lashes, from all my matches, but I am still lavish.

I can see flashes of light, is it my recue? Or is it just an excuse, to be saved.

I must keep my fights standing up right, although, I declare I am not uptight.

I dare you to bring, all of your strikes, because this time it is for my might and not for my sighs, of cries.

I will, always have my pride, shining so bright.

$\mathcal{S}$easons

Seasons of feelings, I can not see healing, feelings! Is what I am made of.

Sometimes I'm happy, but it only seems to be when I am laughing!

I find myself gasping for air, when I am left in despair; it's hard to compare my sadness to anger, because they are both stagger.

My tears! Inflict my fears, of being so alone, as I grow.

It becomes strange, when it comes to my rage; of Un-rightful games.

Seasons to feelings, are quite the same, when it comes to me.

There are days and nights! Of lights and darks, even I don't know what will spark.

The sun is what lifts the day, and the moon usually sets me in the mood, for more than I could have.

The grey sky's, are what make the day stay plain; it is when hide in the shadows of distress.

The rain is meant, to wash the pains away, but it is engraved! Somewhat like the rage inside of me.

One must be brave! To face the seasons, of my days, because I am pain, I am rage, and I gain happiness to madness.

Still I am always game! Whether or not, I stay the same, feelings is who I am! And I am in season.

Closing; with, a Thank you.

I would like to thank god for all my blessings, for giving me the ability, courage and the guidance to write this book, because it would be impossible without him.

I would like to thank my family, for there continued love and support, starting with my parents. Then the crowd my sisters, especially to Yvette for getting me started and encouraging me to follow through with my talent, and Melissa for the idea of this book. I would have not done this without them.

to those i like to call my friends, thank you for being you, for always supporting and for believing in me, you also encourage me to do my best, and never letting me give up.

I dedicate this book to love, and lesson, without taking me out of the box.

About the Author

The author loves to write. She uses music and art in writing and her family is her inspiration. The readers will be interested in reading the book because its poetry in a unique form to where story comes out, its strong and deep but passionately fun with spiritual faith and knowledge so it leaves room for hope and maybe just an artistic experience.

Printed in the United States
By Bookmasters